Books are to be returned on or before
the last

KT-558-165

049626

Race Hate

Anne Rooney

Evans

TITLES IN THE VOICES SERIES:

DRUGS ON THE STREET • GANGS • RACE HATE

RELIGIOUS EXTREMISM • VIOLENCE ON THE SCREEN

Published by Evans Brothers Limited
2A Portman Mansions
Chiltern Street
London W1U 6NR

VISIT OUR WEBSITE
Evans
www.evansbooks.co.uk

First published 2006
© copyright Evans Brothers 2006

British Library Cataloguing in Publication Data
Rooney, Anne
Race hate – (Voices)
1. Racism – Juvenile literature
I.Title
305.8

ISBN 0 237 52717 0
13-digit ISBN (from 1 January 2007)
978 0 237 52717 4

Editor: Susie Brooks
Designer: Mayer Media Ltd
Picture research: Sally Cole

Produced for Evans Brothers Limited by
Monkey Puzzle Media Limited
Gissing's Farm, Fressingfield
Suffolk IP21 5SH, UK

Picture acknowledgements
Photographs were kindly supplied by the following:
African Pictures 14 (Juhan Kuus); Alamy front cover (Frances Roberts), 1 (Ami Vitale), 5 (Photofusion), 10 (David Hoffman Photo Library), 18 (Network Photographers), 24 (Ami Vitale), 27 (Ilse Schrama), 33 (Penny Tweedie), 37 (Nick Cobbing); Corbis 11 (Philip Gould), 23 (Gideon Mendel), 26 (Bettmann), 41 (Scott Houston); David Hoffman Photo Library 28 (Searchlight), 29 (Searchlight), 38; Empics 20 (Elaine Thompson/AP), 25 (John Moore/ AP), 31 (Ali Fraidoon/AP), 32 (PA); Getty Images 7 (AFP), 9 (Hulton Archive), 12 (Time Life Pictures), 13 (AFP), 15 (AFP), 17 (Marco Di Lauro), 39 (David Brauchli), 40, 42 (Kareem Black); Network Photographers 6 (Jenny Matthews); Reuters 30 (Mian Khursheed), 43 (Mike Hutchings); Rex Features 8 (Action Press), 16 (TS/ Keystone USA), 19 (SIPA), 34 (George Sweeney), 36 (Paul Cooper); Topfoto.co.uk 4, 21, 22, 35.

CONTENTS

WHAT IS RACE?

How do we define race? Are people with different coloured skin – or different features – much the same as you, or very different?

Advertising for Benetton clothing highlights the fact that although people of different races may vary in appearance, we are all very similar as human beings.

Personal matter

Many people believe that different groups of people – such as white, black and Asian people – have different racial characteristics besides their appearance. Race is not just about physical features. It is part of our cultural identity; it may affect how we feel about ourselves and others, and how we live. Gabriella, a white European, prefers to be with other white people:

❝ Humanity is divided into lots of different races. We're all different, not just in the colour of our skin. It's quite natural to want to stick with your own kind. I'd rather spend my time with other white people – I have more in common with them. ❞

Colour and race need be no barrier to friendship and fun. Many people gain a lot from mixed-race relationships.

Willing to mix

Scientists have found no major genetic differences between people of different races and no genes that distinguish racial group. Many people would be happy to mix with others from all places, and of all colours and ethnic backgrounds, but they can't always do so. David, a rabbi in Brooklyn, New York, USA, says of Hasidic Jews and Caribbeans:

❝ We realised that, even though we had lived together for 20 years, we knew almost nothing about each other. ❞

Angelo lives in an area of the USA where different groups tend to keep to themselves. He thinks he probably has a lot in common with people from other backgrounds, such as the Albanian families that live nearby. He says:

❝ I'd really like to get to know some Albanian kids. We should get along OK – we're more alike than different. After all, we all face the same problems as teenagers. ❞

"Race... is a social and political construct.... It has no basis in science.... The mapping of the human genome could be pivotal in promoting the concept of one race, the human race."
Harold P Freeman, MD, Celera (one organisation involved in mapping the human genome).

WHY DOES RACE MATTER?

Even if there is no scientific basis to race, we have made race matter. People have acted for thousands of years as though those who look different are different. And many people feel different, too.

Racial pride

Throughout history, people have been enslaved and abused, driven from land they occupy and treated as less than human – all because of their race. But in spite of all this, most people take pride in their race and their heritage. Beninah, a teenager from New York, explains what being African American means to her:

❝ I'm proud to be black – African American. We are descended from kings and queens. Africa was the cradle of civilisation. We made mathematics, medicine, science and language long before Europeans. ❞

At Notting Hill Carnival in London, UK, Caribbean people lead celebrations enjoyed by everyone.

Many Roma people from Kosovo have tried to flee their country. These refugees hoped to settle in Greece, but after spending months in a camp they were turned away.

Better than the rest?

Seeing differences between your 'own' people and others can lead to an 'us and them' attitude. Some people think they are better than those of other races. Early white settlers in Africa, Australia and the Americas felt superior to the local people because Europeans had a technologically developed culture. They called the locals 'savages' and 'barbarians'. Now, people pick on different characteristics they think they see in other races.

Imre lives in Slovakia, where the Roma people suffer a lot of hatred and distrust. He says:

❝ Most Roma are lazy. They live off the state, having loads of children so they can get social benefits. They don't try to help themselves, so they live in social misery. ❞

Beliefs like this make it hard for Slavs and Romas to live together.

"Notions of racial and cultural superiority, bolstered by pseudo-scientific ideas of racial hierarchies, [have] served to justify colonisation (just as they were used to defend slavery)."
Andrew Geddes, *The Politics of Immigration and Race*, 1996.

WHY HATE OTHER RACES?

People may resent other races if they think that they personally are losing out to them, or see them as a threat, or dislike different ways of life that they associate with another race.

Forging views

Some people hold racist views that are based purely in ignorance – they may criticise people they know nothing about, or turn dislike of one person into anger towards an entire race. Others extend their disapproval of a country's political or religious stance to individuals. Carrie, a teenager in St Louis, USA, says:

❝ Anyone who looks as though they might be Arab or Middle Eastern, I steer clear of them. I'm frightened of them and they hate us. ❞

Yvonne, from Canada, declares of her neighbouring country:

❝ America is extremely arrogant, knows nothing of the world outside itself and wants to tell everyone what to do. I hate Americans. ❞

Palestinians and Israelis have fought over ownership of the land that is now Israel for many years. The hatred involved in the conflict often reveals itself in suicide bombings, such as this one in Jerusalem.

In the early and mid-twentieth century, white people often disregarded black people completely. Many white families employed black workers to serve them.

VICTIMS

A survey in Canada found that:

30%	of black people
21%	of South Asian people
18%	of Chinese people

had experienced occasional or frequent racism in the last five years.

Accepting stereotypes

People may have racist ideas instilled in them from an early age and never question them. Often, they accept stereotypes without thinking for themselves. A stereotype is a 'typical' picture of a group of people. People who are treated as though they match a stereotype are upset by it. Ben is a black student in Texas, USA. He says:

❝ White people are always thinking I'm a criminal, waiting for me to do something – hit them or steal from a shop. They're always watching me. ❞

WHO NEEDS A REASON?

For some people, just the fact that someone else is different is reason enough for hating or hitting out at them. How do they justify their acts?

Making colour matter

It's easy to lose sight of what we have in common as people once we let differences take over. Some people say they abuse others just because they 'don't like their colour'. Sean, for example, lives in New York, USA. He and his friends pick on Mexicans for no reason:

" When there's nothing to do, we go out and get racial against Mexicans.... If we see a Mexican, even if they're not doing anything to bother us, we beat them up. "

In Manchester, UK, Robert threatened to nail-bomb 'all the non-white areas'. He later murdered an Asian man, Zahid, in their shared prison cell.

"I am convinced that had Zahid been white, he would not have died."
Trevor Phillips, chair of the Commission for Racial Equality, UK.

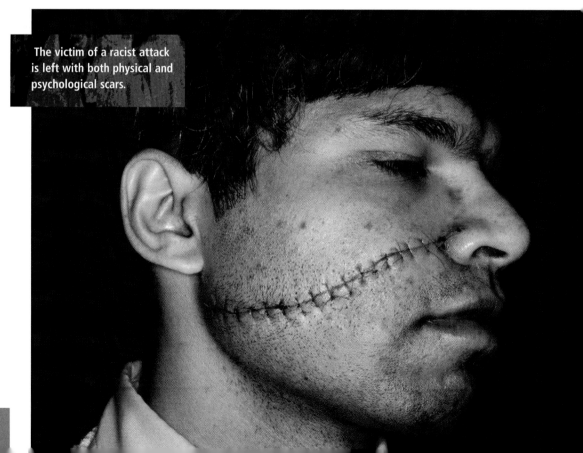

The victim of a racist attack is left with both physical and psychological scars.

Forgetting humanity

Black American Wilbert Rideau murdered a white woman for no reason other than, he says, 'because I was dangerous'. He explains how his hatred of white people blinded him to his victim's humanity until he, too, had to plead for his life:

❝ The fact that I hated white people added an extra dimension to the whole affair. I mean, you're not that concerned about the humanity of people you hate.... [Being sentenced to death] made me realise what my victim must have felt, because I did the same thing to her. I ignored her pleas. ❞

Wilbert Rideau was sentenced to death for killing a white bank clerk in a bungled robbery. He was released after 44 years in prison.

FBI FIGURES ON HATE CRIME, 2003

Of 7,462 hate crimes in the USA, almost 50% were racially motivated.

	% OF HATE CRIME PERPETRATORS	% OF US POPULATION
White	61.8%	69.1%
Black	21.8%	12.9%
Hispanic	14.6%	12.5%
Asian	1.2%	4.2%
Native American/ Alaskan	0.6%	1.5%

DOES THE PAST MATTER?

Much of the world's racial tension is rooted in the past. African Americans know, for example, that their ancestors suffered slavery and other injustices at the hands of whites. Can this explain hatred today?

Looking back

Until the mid-twentieth century, black people in America and South Africa were segregated – forced to use separate facilities to keep them apart from white people. In South Africa this was called apartheid and continued until 1991.

In the USA, the Black Power movement in the 1960s won legal equality for black Americans, but anger erupted into violent rioting in the 1970s and 80s. Paulina, an African American, says:

❝ Do you think we're going to just forget what white people have done to us? We were treated like the scum of the Earth, like animals – worse than that. If you'd only been through half of it you would respect us African Americans! ❞

Black workers in South Africa travelled in black-only buses from the poor townships where they were forced to live until 1991.

Martin Luther King inspired and led black people in the USA in their fight for equality with whites. He was assassinated in 1968.

Moving on

White people living in America now are not responsible for slavery and injustices that happened before they were born. Segregation in the USA and apartheid in South Africa are over. Dwelling on the past fuels resentment. Karl, who lives in Canada, says:

No white man today should have to feel bad about slavery or slaughtered Indians. I am German – my people murdered millions of Jews during the Second World War. I don't feel guilty because I committed no crime.

Graham, from Illinois, USA, is more abrupt:

They still moan about the slave trade – it ended hundreds of years ago! Get with the times, and stop using it as an excuse not to work and to get free money.

WHO OWNS THE LAND?

Black people have always lived in Africa, but since Europeans settled there, blacks have struggled with whites over ownership of the land. Should black people reclaim the territory that belonged to their ancestors?

Colonial days

In the eighteenth and nineteenth centuries, white people from Europe settled in Africa and took over the land. African countries became colonies of European nations. Now colonialism has ended and African countries are again under black rule, but many black Africans want white people to leave. Mehereta lives in Eritrea, eastern Africa. She says:

❝ If whites aren't happy living under African rule, they can leave our lands. We would be better off with more leaders like Mugabe [President of Zimbabwe], who support black people with courage.... We don't need those who look after the interests of the white overlords, who took our land and oppressed our people. ❞

South African residents, who had seized land belonging to white farmers, return to a township to reconsider their position after the land they took was surrounded by police and soldiers.

WHO OWNS ZIMBABWE?

Zimbabwe has a population of around 12 million, of which 98% is black and less than 1% white.

White farmers own nearly 50% of the land.

Black families typically farm 3 hectares each.

The average white farm is 2,000 hectares.

A white farmer in Zimbabwe stands amid the ruins of his burnt-out house, which was destroyed by aggressive black 'war veterans'.

White rights?

Many white people in Africa were born there. They see no reason to leave and no reason for their fellow Africans to hate them. Mike is a white farmer in Zimbabwe, southern Africa. His farm has been attacked many times by black militants known as 'war veterans'. He says:

❝ We are Zimbabweans. We have been accepted as Zimbabweans all our lives. And why should we leave? We have nowhere else to go, we have no other home and our families are here with us. Why should we be expected to leave purely because we are white? We are Zimbabweans, and we fully intend to stay here. ❞

Many white farmers, however, have already left – and others have been killed or have had their farms seized by black aggressors.

'WHY DON'T THEY JUST GO HOME'?

Immigration – the movement of people into one country from another – is a common cause of conflict, particularly in Europe. Do people have a right to stop foreigners moving into their area?

Bringing a burden?

People often consider their way of life threatened by outsiders with different lifestyles. Many complain that immigrants cause unemployment, or live on social benefits paid for by long-term residents. Belgian politician Filip Dewinter says:

“ Most immigrants are not integrating. They are sticking together in ghettos around the smell of their own food and their own way of life.... They should behave like we do. ”

Trevor, from Alabama, USA, has a similar attitude:

“ I'm sick of hearing of these damn wet backs [Mexicans] coming in to the US packed like sardines in a Honda. Dump them back in Mexico – we don't need them in our land. ”

Many cities in North America and Europe have a Chinatown district in which Chinese families live and work as they might in China.

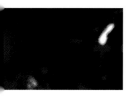

A better life?

People move to other countries for many reasons. It may be to escape oppression in their homeland, or to seek a better standard of living. Host countries may welcome skilled immigrants if there is a skills shortage. The USA and Australia have both used systems to limit immigration to people who will be 'useful' to society. But unskilled workers may meet resentment and even violence. Yassin, from Morocco, northern Africa, went to live in Belgium. He encountered problems:

❝ At the job centre I often saw staff write 'doesn't want Moroccans' as they took job descriptions on the phone. In the street, I am spat at. I have had dog mess pushed through my door. All I want is a decent job to raise my family, but they don't want us here. ❞

Illegal immigrants trying to enter Europe from Africa wait to take refuge in a camp in Italy before being sent back to Africa.

WHAT LIMITS?

PEOPLE LIVING IN THE RUSSIAN FEDERATION WHO WANT

LIMITS IMPOSED ON IMMIGRANTS

46%	want limits on	Caucasians
39%	want limits on	Chinese/Vietnamese
15%	want limits on	Jews
14%	want limits on	'all except Russians'
21%	feel there is no need for restrictions	

Neprikosnovenniy zapas, 2004

"The fact that [Muslim Europeans] are still thought of as immigrants means we have a big, big problem. They're born here. They pay their taxes. They speak the languages. They are not guests in the European house; they're co-owners."

Carl Devos, professor of political science, Ghent University, Belgium.

IS THERE A WRONG PART OF TOWN?

Often, people of a particular racial or ethnic group settle together in one area of a city or country. They enjoy living amongst people who share their traditions and way of life. Need this lead to conflict?

Inside looking out

Living in a close-knit community gives many people a sense of security and belonging. They may feel wary of others whose ways are unfamiliar to them or incompatible with their own. Feyzi is a young Albanian man living in New York, USA. He describes how Albanians live together:

&& It's a closed community. A lot of people think we're strange, because we live like we did in the old country. We learn that the only people we can trust are ourselves – other Albanians – so we stick together. &&

Ashu, of the Jarawa tribe in Indonesia, puts it simply:

&& My world is in the forest. Your world is outside. We don't like people from outside. &&

Flowers are laid at the scene of racist attacks against a Turkish community in Germany.

Members of a black street gang pose in Los Angeles, USA. Fights over territory between rival gangs often become very violent.

KEEP OUT!

PERCENTAGE OF PEOPLE 'RESISTANT' TO IMMIGRANTS MOVING INTO THEIR COUNTRY

Greece	87%
Hungary	86%
Austria	64%
Portugal	62%
Finland	59%
Luxembourg	53%
UK	51%
Denmark, Czech Republic, Spain	50%
East Germany	48%

European Social Survey 2002–03, European Monitoring Centre on Racism and Xenophobia

Defending territory

When a group believes an area or neighbourhood is 'theirs', they may feel the need to defend it against outsiders. People who are seen as not belonging may be driven out, even if they are not doing any harm – just being there means they're 'looking for trouble'. This can be a trigger or excuse for racial violence. Salvatore lives in an Italian area of Brooklyn, New York, USA. He describes how he and his group of friends behave:

❝ Sometimes when we're hanging out, doing nothing, someone will suggest we go look for people who don't belong here. Sometimes, we go look for blacks to jump [attack]. Sometimes we're not so fussed and we jump anyone who looks like they aren't meant to be on our turf. ❞

WHY DOES RACISM TURN TO VIOLENCE?

It is possible to resent, fear or even hate a group without turning to violence. So why does race hate – like other sources of conflict – so often end in aggression against individuals?

The aggressive approach of many racist demonstrators, such as this skinhead at a UK pro-white rally, can quickly turn to violence.

A quick thrill

Some people commit racist attacks to go along with what their friends are doing, or they decide to 'teach someone a lesson' or act out of boredom. Others want to prove themselves, look tough or show off. Nicky, 17, carried out a violent attack on Mukhtar, an Asian man in London, UK. A national newspaper described it as:

❝ ...an attack whose only motivations were a quick, vicious thrill and the glorification of a stupid gang. ❞

Nicky's ex-girlfriend comments:

❝ He was mild and meek, like his dad, but he wanted to be accepted by his friends. To be accepted, he did the attack. Now in his community, he's someone really hard. ❞

Racist abuse can lead to further violence in the form of retaliation. This attack on a white man took place after a pro-white rally targeted blacks and Asians.

> **"Racism is an attack on the very notion of universal human rights. It systematically denies certain people their full human rights because of their colour, race, ethnicity, descent or national origin."**
> Human Rights Watch, 2003.

Chain reaction

Racism can quickly spiral into increasing violence. A racist comment, for example, can provoke anger that gets out of control. Some people choose violence as a form of self-defence – Karon, a Nyoongar Aboriginal in Australia, gives an example:

❝ When I was 14, this boy called me a half-caste boong. So I grabbed him and I hit his head against a brick wall. ❞

Some people attack to defend others. Greg, a white boy in Los Angeles, USA, describes how he reacted when his friend was stabbed by black youths. Greg was stopped by the police before he hit anyone – but his intention had been to take revenge:

❝ Yesterday my best friend was stabbed by some blacks in the parking lot. He drove off to the hospital. When I heard, I took my Boston Red Sox bat and went to the lot and I looked for those black kids. ❞

IS IT EVER 'JUST A LAUGH'?

Many attacks seem minor – teasing, name–calling or a bit of pushing about. Everyone suffers taunting and minor harassment occasionally. Is it any different if it picks up on racial characteristics?

Damaging property 'for a joke' can destroy someone's livelihood. This man's restaurant has been wrecked in a petty racist assault.

Bully tactics

People who tease and bully often say victims take it too seriously – that the racist element is incidental. They use this as an excuse to get away with hurtful abuse. Neil, a football fan from Liverpool, UK, describes how a black player was treated:

❝ We were playing against a team with a black player... some guys started to throw bananas at him, like he was a monkey. It was quite funny, really. It's not just racism – they throw sweets at fat people, too. ❞

No joke

Attackers pick on features that mark someone as different – a Muslim headscarf or Rastafarian dreadlocks, for example. An attack can be really unpleasant and frightening for the victim. It's not a laugh for them. Kate, a white teenager from London, UK, describes how a young Muslim girl was the victim of a 'happy slapping' attack:

❝ One girl pulled off her headscarf and was pushing her around and laughing at her, calling her names. The other girl was filming it on her mobile phone and laughing. The poor Muslim girl was really upset. They didn't hurt her physically very much, but it was really terrible to her to have her head uncovered. She was trying to cover herself up, and crying. ❞

A teacher helps to resolve a racist dispute between her pupils. In school, race or colour is often used as an excuse to pick on someone. Racist bullying may involve physical violence or verbal abuse.

"Children and young people called about racial harassment involving phone calls and letters, graffiti, verbal abuse in the streets and at the house, stone throwing, wrecked possessions, broken windows and fireworks through the letterbox."

Childline, UK charity offering phone support to children who suffer abuse.

WHAT ABOUT THE WIDER WORLD?

Racist attacks don't affect just individuals on a small scale. In the wider world, the effects of race hate can be catastrophic for whole populations.

Ongoing terror

Wars, ethnic cleansing, terrorism and genocide may all have their roots in racial hatred. Race hate develops quickly from political and religious disputes. A rabbi in Israel says:

❝ Palestinians have no place on this land. Never! If we must kill every Palestinian to keep our land free, we will do so. ❞

Jozo lives in a village in Bosnia. He describes a race riot that erupted between Bosnian and Serbian residents:

❝ Everyone was throwing rocks, punching people and hitting each other with sticks or whatever they could find. Serbs and Bosniaks will never get along. There is still too much tension there, too much hate. ❞

A Serbian woman grieves for a relative killed with other Serbs in Kosovo during the ethnic conflict in Bosnia-Herzegovina.

Global impact

International and political events can have an impact on people far from the area directly affected. Since the attacks by Muslims on New York's World Trade Center in September 2001, and on London, UK, in July 2005, Middle Eastern people living in Europe and the USA have suffered suspicion, hatred and abuse. Americans and Europeans in the Middle East have been attacked for their race, too. Ramazan, 16, is Iranian but now lives in the Netherlands. He describes the kind of assault that people who look Arab or Muslim often suffer:

❝ In the shopping mall with my sister, some skinheads attacked us. They pulled at my sister's clothes and made lewd remarks to her. Then they punched me and hit me with a baseball bat. They said we were towel-head, terrorist scum. ❞

A prisoner gestures from his solitary confinement cage in Abu Ghraib, Iraq. Abuse of Iraqi detainees by Western troops has led to retaliatory attacks.

"There is no doubt that incidents impacting on the Muslim community have increased [since the London suicide bombings]."

Tarique Ghaffur, Metropolitan Police Assistant Commissioner in the UK.

CAN A RACE BE 'PURE'?

Some ethnic groups want to keep their community 'pure' and don't allow marriage outside the group. Taken to extremes, ideas of racial purity can lead to mass slaughter.

Assuming ideals

In Nazi Germany, Hitler wanted a 'master race' of Aryan Germans – a tall, blonde, blue-eyed Nordic type. Jews, Roma people and others who didn't fit the ideal were killed. Modern neo-Nazi groups echo Hitler's beliefs. William Pierce, a founder member of the US group the National Alliance, says:

❝ Many otherwise knowledgeable and hard-headed Americans just can't entertain the idea of rounding up the Jews and getting rid of them, even when the situation is as urgent as it is in America today. And really, in the long run, that is the only way to solve the Jewish problem. ❞

Black workers peacefully campaign to be treated as human beings as they march past soldiers aiming bayonets in Memphis, USA, in 1968.

This war cemetery in Sarajevo is testament to ethnic cleansing in Bosnia-Herzegovina.

"Throughout the [Second World War], public opinion polls showed 10–13 percent of the American public consistently supporting the annihilation or extermination of the Japanese as a people."

John Dower, *War Without Mercy*.

Ethnic cleansing

Genetic control of a population is called eugenics. The USA had a secret policy to sterilise 'undesirable' people from 1907 to 1979. In the last 20 years of the programme, most victims were black. Christine was sterilised without her knowledge after giving birth at the age of 15. She found out years later. She says:

❝ I felt like I was worthless, less than a person. The people that did this took my soul. The authorities are just waiting for us all to die out, so the problem goes away. They don't want to face up to what they did. ❞

The more direct way to control the racial mix is to kill a whole population.

KILLED FOR RACE

VICTIMS OF KILLING TO ENSURE 'RACIAL PURITY', 1900–2000

VICTIMS	WHERE	DATE	NUMBER
Jews	Germany	1933–45	6,000,000
Armenians	Turkey	1915–23	around 1,500,000
Tutsis	Rwanda	1994	800,000
Roma	Germany	1933–45	500,000
Bosnian Muslims	Bosnia-Herzegovina	1992–95	200,000

ARE RACIST FUN AND GAMES OK?

Racial hatred infiltrates all areas of our lives, even music, films and computer games. But violence is often presented as entertainment. Is it any different if race is the subject?

Violent games

In the computer game Ethnic Cleansing, players can dress in Ku Klux Klan robes or as skinheads and, as the advertising says:

> **Run through the ghetto blasting away various blacks and spics [Hispanics] in an attempt to gain entrance to the subway... where the Jews have hidden to avoid the carnage. Then if you're lucky you can blow away Jews as they scream, 'Oy Vey!', on your way to their command centre.**

Some people defend this by declaring it is a fantasy land, not reality. Playing the game, they say, is committing no crime nor creating a conspiracy.

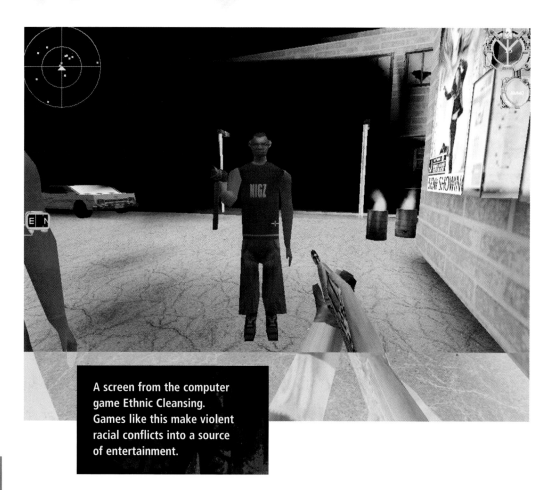

A screen from the computer game Ethnic Cleansing. Games like this make violent racial conflicts into a source of entertainment.

The Swedish band Nibelungen give a Nazi salute during a gig. White Power music is performed by racist groups all around the world.

"Racist music is principally derived from the far-right skinhead movement and, through the Internet, this music has become perhaps the most important tool of the international neo-Nazi movement to gain revenue and new recruits."
Human Rights and Equal Opportunities Commission, Australia, 2002.

Real victims

Members of the groups portrayed as victims in games like Ethnic Cleansing are angry, saying that they encourage real violence and race hate. In most violent computer games, the player has nothing personal against the victim, but in racist games the player is invited to act out real-world hate. Darren Schneider, president of a Jewish Student Union, says:

❝ It just jumps out at me as something that people shouldn't even go check out. To have a game that glorifies this act is sickening. Creativity of this nature should be condemned. ❞

The marketing for the games targets teenagers and young men, who many people feel are most likely to act on feelings of hatred.

WHO ELSE CAN WE BLAME?

Issues of race and race hate are covered by the media and discussed frequently by politicians. Does media coverage influence the way ordinary people think about race?

Biased reports?

The way stories – both real and fictional – are presented by the media may appear to favour one group over another. Anmar, from Iraq, lives in Sweden. He thinks views of Middle Eastern people are influenced by how they are depicted on television. He recounts:

❝ A lot of the time, we're shown as spivs, or criminals. Arabs are shown as dirty people who don't treat women well – never normal characters who just happen to be from the Middle East. ❞

Callum, a white boy from New York, USA, says the way news is chosen encourages racism, too:

❝ When something happens to a black guy, the news hypes it up. They don't do anything when a white person gets jumped. No one cares about white people any more, they're not news. ❞

Students at an Islamic religious school in Pakistan demonstrate against a crackdown on their activities after the London suicide bombings, 2005.

President George W Bush talks to US troops in the Middle East. Must war between nations lead to racism between individuals?

Reading between the lines

When a country is in conflict with another, both politicians and the media may demonise the opponent. If people get to know individuals of another race, they may be surprised to find how much they have in common. Gary fought in the Gulf War, 1990–91. He says:

❝ When you're out there, you see the people fighting are no different from you. They've got a family, they want to go home. And you want to go home. It was a shock. We were all told we were doing this for our country and that these people were all terrible, every one of them. But then you're out there and you realise, they're not terrible, they're just like me. ❞

"Whenever politicians make speeches about tides and waves of immigrants which threaten to engulf us, to swamp us, you can be sure that attacks will follow close behind."

The Howard League for Penal Reform, UK.

SET UP TO FAIL?

It is common for some racial groups to be accused of being lazy and criminal – a set of people who do little but get into trouble. But is criminal activity really linked with race?

A fair deal?

Certain ethnic groups are seen by many people to be thieves, cheats and abusers of the social benefit system. Being lazy and criminal is a charge often levelled at black people in the USA. Jimmy, a white American, says:

" It would be harder for whites to claim to be more civilised than blacks if blacks didn't act like savages. They're killing each other, doing drugs, having illegitimate children, and landing in prison all the time. "

Figures for imprisonment may even support this view – proportionally, more black Americans than white are jailed and executed. But many people think this is because they are not given a fair deal in court, or that disadvantage leads them into crime.

In the USA, black people stand a higher chance of being searched by police, and arrested, than white people.

"The continuing sufferings of indigenous Australians [Aboriginals] are undoubtedly our greatest and most long-standing shame – and the deprivations endured by the children are the very worst aspect of that shame."

Australian Federal Court judge, Justice Marcus Einfeld.

An Australian Aboriginal family gather by their home – a hut made of bark. With such a poor start in life, it is hard for many Aboriginals to rise above disadvantage.

Give us a chance

In Australia, the indigenous Aboriginal people have been killed and oppressed for centuries – they were not even counted as 'people' until the 1960s. White settlers took their land and forcibly removed Aboriginal children to be raised by white families or in orphanages. Aboriginal people now have high levels of poverty, unemployment, crime and alcoholism. Their failure in society leads to victimisation and hatred from some white Australians. Richard, an Aboriginal man, has little hope that it will ever change:

❝ We are second-class citizens in our own country. Most Aboriginal people will never get anywhere. We have no education, job advancement or self-respect. We are a race set aside, abused, accused and all bundled into one no matter what we do. ❞

DOES AFFIRMATIVE ACTION WORK?

Affirmative action involves giving people special benefits to help them overcome difficulties caused by racism in the past or present. But does it make racial tension worse?

A helping hand

The aim of affirmative action is to help disadvantaged people achieve more in life. Institutions and employers in countries including the USA, New Zealand and parts of Europe, are required by law to give opportunities to groups who may otherwise be discriminated against. Consuela is a young Hispanic woman who was able to go to university as a result of affirmative action. She says:

" I was an immigrant kid from New Mexico. I could never have gone to college without affirmative action. Hispanics rarely say what affirmative action has done for them as they feel it's a negative thing. But we need to be clear and honest about its success. "

For immigrants who fail to find work in their host country, like this Arab woman in France, the unhappy alternative may be begging on the streets.

David Dinkins was
the first black mayor
of New York, USA.
Many black people
were encouraged by
his success.

Disadvantaging others?

People who don't themselves benefit from affirmative action often feel that
their own chances are reduced by it. Some see it as bias against white people
– if the law favoured whites, they say, it would be attacked as racism. Some
black people oppose affirmative action, too. Luther, a black Californian, sees
it as confirming white ideas of black inferiority. He declares:

**❝ It's time to set the past aside now. We don't need
special treatment as victims because of what
happened to our ancestors.... Racial quotas,
affirmative action programs – all that is just making
things worse. Whites resent them and they reinforce
beliefs in black inferiority. It's not keeping pace with
the multiethnic society we have now, it's outdated. ❞**

**"It is irrelevant whether a government's racial
classifications are drawn by those who wish to
oppress a race or by those who have a sincere desire
to help those thought to be disadvantaged. In each
instance, it is racial discrimination, plain and simple."**

Black US judge Justice Clarence Thomas ruling against discriminating
in favour of contractors who hire workers from minority groups.

RACISM AGAINST WHITES?

Some white people feel strongly that they are being treated unfairly – that too many advantages are now given to other racial groups. Do they have a right to protest?

LA FRANCE RETROUVÉE

Fighting for rights

In the USA, Europe and Australia, people calling themselves 'white supremacists' or 'white nationalists' argue that white people are unfairly losing out to non-white groups and are not allowed to complain about it. Harry, a white man in the USA, says:

❝ White Americans are supposed to see the flood of Hispanics and Asians as a cultural benefit. We're supposed to 'celebrate' our own loss of influence, our dispossession in our own land. We don't even have a right to speak out against it or we're called racist. ❞

The issue of freedom of speech is difficult. Should people be refused the right to voice their views in case it offends others?

Jean Marie le Pen, president of the right-wing French National Front, has taken a firm stand against immigration. He has enjoyed popularity that has worried people with a more liberal view of racial issues in France.

White supremacists often use their national flag to reinforce their message that they are 'defending' their country.

Seeking control

Many white supremacists do not want just equality with other groups – they want to put white people in control again and leave other groups disadvantaged. Their activities often stir up race hate. In 2001, riots in Bradford, in the UK, started after a rally by the National Front, a right-wing, pro-white organisation. Kyle, who works monitoring racial attacks, says:

66 The National Front targets areas where most people are lower-middle class whites. They foster fear in the community by saying immigrants are taking local jobs, living on benefit, swamping English culture. Then they go round recruiting angry young people to beat up blacks and Asians. 99

"Freedom of speech is not an unqualified principle. If it results in this kind of anarchy and mayhem [Bradford race riots] as a direct reaction to the presence of the far-right, then we have to go back to the drawing board."
Shahid Malik, Commission for Racial Equality, UK.

WHAT ARE RACE HATE GROUPS?

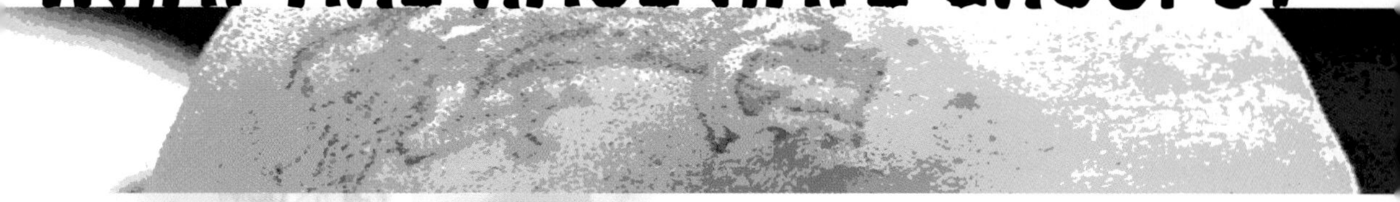

Racist groups often form when people see their way of life threatened. They might meet in the real world, or share views and ideas on the Internet. What are their aims?

Defending a cause

A race hate group is one that undermines or harms another particular group of people. Members of the groups believe they are righting wrongs committed against them. They claim they have the right to do this and that their aims are positive. Davis Wolfgang Hawke founded an American pro-white group. He explains the reasons for starting the group:

❝ Who are we?.... We're white men who refuse to stand idly by as our race gets gobbled up by the hordes of traitors, Jews and immigrants who seek to wipe us out. We're... ready to take back our nation for the cause of racial preservation. ❞

Their claim is that they want a fair deal – just as black and Hispanic people have asked for a fair deal.

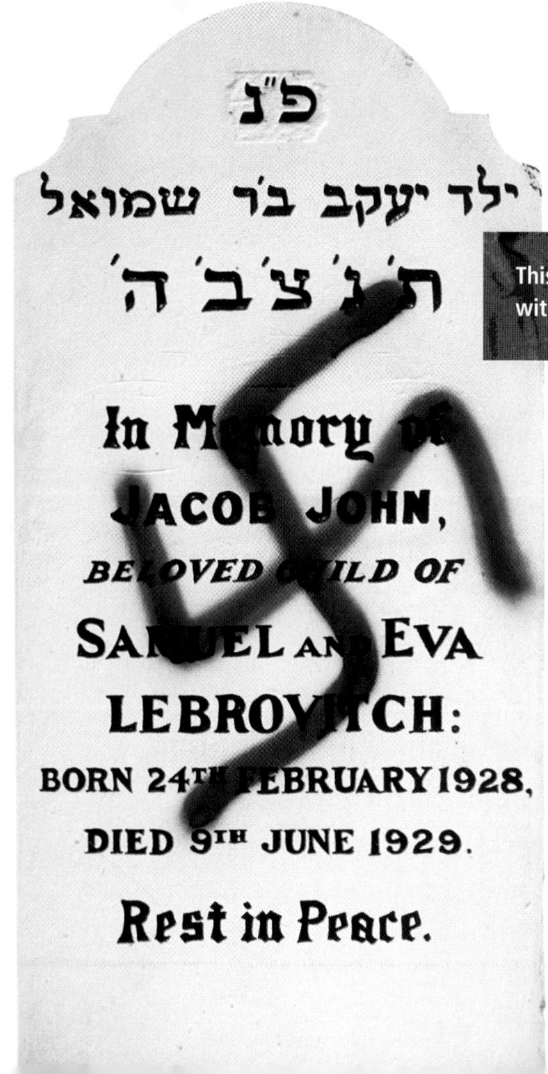

This Jewish baby's gravestone has been daubed with a Nazi swastika by racists.

פ"נ

ילד יעקב ב'ר שמואל

ת'נ'צ'ב'ה'

In Memory of JACOB JOHN, BELOVED CHILD OF SAMUEL and EVA LEBROVITCH: BORN 24TH FEBRUARY 1928, DIED 9TH JUNE 1929.

Rest in Peace.

HATE STATES

US States with the Most Race Hate Groups

State	Known Active Race Hate Groups in 2004
South Carolina	47
Florida	43
California	42
Georgia	41
Texas	40

Southern Poverty Law Center

Turning to violence

Race hate groups often gain support when people feel economically worse off and look for someone to blame. They frequently target the young – young men who feel alienated and failed by society are often persuaded to blame other racial groups for their problems. Groups may use violence rather than seeking a legal, peaceful solution to the problems they see.

Alexei, a member of the Russian neo-Nazi group Schultz88, talks about their plans to remove ethnic minority groups from Russia. He says:

❝ [We are] a white man's al–Qaeda. We don't care how many [ethnic minorities] end up dead. The more, the better. The time of our jihad has come.... We don't consider ourselves Russian. We belong to the white race! ❞

Schultz88 and groups like it have become increasingly popular in Russia as economic conditions have become worse.

A skinhead attends a nationalist rally in Moscow, Russia. Tattoos are often a badge of nationalist groups.

"People don't see [neo-Nazism], but it's here and it kills."
Vyacheslav Sukhachev, professor of sociology at the University of St. Petersburg, Russia.

CAN WE CONTROL ONLINE HATE?

The Internet is used more and more to spread racist materials and bring racists together. Should we try to control online racist groups, or do people have a right to air their views, however offensive they may be?

Unbounded territory

In some countries, it is illegal to spread racist material and express racist ideas. The Internet is not constrained by national boundaries. More and more race hate websites and online groups are run from countries that have no laws to control them. Adrián Jmelnizky investigates racial abuse cases in Argentina. He says:

❝ We could try to act against the companies hosting these sites, but the legislation just isn't there to take action against them. Internet use is beyond the scope of the anti-discrimination law. ❞

Matt Hale, leader of the white supremacist group World Church of the Creator, shares his views on the web.

A modern Ku Klux Klan 'knight' gives a Nazi salute. The Ku Klux Klan is trying to increase its membership using the Internet.

Freedom of speech

People who form or join a racist group online feel they should be free to express their views, and that people who don't like the views should not read them. The Ku Klux Klan is an infamous organisation in the USA responsible for killing thousands of black people in the twentieth century. It still has many active groups throughout the USA, and a website and message boards online. It defends its website, saying:

❝ This page is entirely political in nature. If you do not agree with our politics that is fine. Just remember that we have every right to express our opinions. This is in the interest of free speech and to combat Internet censorship. ❞

"What was proscribed, undercover, shameful and liable to prosecution in the past is today readily available and viewable on the net.... Movements which were in decline in both Europe and the USA have received a new lease of life thanks to the sites they have created."

European Commission against Racism and Intolerance.

IS THERE A WAY FORWARD?

More and more people are moving to different countries. Will we learn to live peacefully, even happily, with people from different backgrounds? Or will tension and hatred only increase?

Taking a stand

Many perpetrators of racial abuse act through fear of making a fuss – they are scared of becoming victims themselves. Others just do what their friends are doing without actually thinking about the consequences. Taking a stand might mean arguing a case or choosing to be with different people. Stephen used to be a member of a racist group. He now works with young people in London, UK. He says:

“ I tell the kids I used to be in a racist political group. I tell them what it does, and why that's wrong. They blame the lack of jobs, the lack of housing, low benefits – all that – on immigrants and asylum seekers. I've told them it was way worse in the Great Depression, in the 1930s. But there were hardly any black people here in those days, so it wasn't their fault then and it's not their fault now. It's an economic problem, and not a race problem. ”

Racial tensions can easily get out of hand. Trying to stop a fight may not be easy, but taking a stand against racism could help to prevent conflict in the first place.

If enough people reject racism, can we all live together harmoniously?

WON'T MIX

A survey in Canada found that:

1 in 10 people would not welcome a next-door neighbour of a different race

13% of people would never consider a relationship or marriage with someone of a different race.

"We hold these truths to be self-evident, that all men are created equal..."

US Declaration of Independence, 1776.

Changing minds

Affirmative action and legislation to prevent racist behaviour may help. But we also need to change the attitudes of ordinary people to defeat racism. Some people forge friendships with those from different backgrounds but find they are bullied or criticised for it. Ben, a schoolchild in the UK, tells how an older boy bullied him:

❝ He pushed me and called me names.... He just said, 'Why are you hanging around with a black [swearword]?' So I said, 'Because he's my best friend,' and he went, 'Well you're stupid.' ❞

Other people experience great joy in multi-cultural relationships. Marion, from Sweden, says racism can be beaten with a bit of effort:

❝ I treat everyone the same.... I don't call people names due to their skin colour and do not expect to be treated any different or called names because of mine. You don't ask to be born a certain colour. At the end of the day we are all people and if we were to treat each other as such, maybe racism could die out. ❞

TIMELINE

1479   The Spanish first take black slaves from Africa.

1562   The British slave trade with Africa begins.

1619   Black people are taken from Africa to work as slaves on plantations in the USA and the West Indies.

1622–1900s Indigenous North American people are annihilated through genocide, war and slavery. Estimates of those killed range up to 12 million.

1833   The Slavery Abolition Act ends slavery in the UK and British colonies.

1865   Slavery is abolished in the USA at the end of the American Civil War.

1880s–1960s 'Jim Crow' laws enforce segregation of black and white people in the USA, with black people having to use different facilities in all areas of life.

1882–1968 Mobs in the USA kill 4,743 people in lynchings. Over 70 per cent of the victims are black.

1901   The Australian constitution denies citizenship, the vote and the right to military duty to Aboriginal people, Asians and Africans.

1904   The First Aboriginal Act gives the Chief Protector rights of guardianship over Aboriginal and half-caste children in Western Australia, replacing their parents as legal guardians.

1910   Afrikaners take over governing South Africa, effectively starting the separation of black and white people that would be called 'apartheid' from 1948.

1915–1923 Turks kill around 1.5 million Armenians living in Turkey.

1915–1970s Aboriginal children are forcibly removed from their parents, many to act as servants to white Australians. Around one third of Aboriginal children are affected.

1934   The Aborigines Act allows Aboriginal Australians to apply to 'stop being Aborigines' and to enjoy the same rights as white people.

1939–1945 More than 10 million people die in Nazi death camps as Hitler implements a policy of racial purity, killing Jews, Romas, Poles and other 'undesirables'.

1948 The Universal Declaration of Human Rights acknowledges the equality of all people, regardless of race.

1955 Martin Luther King starts the US black rights movement. Action occurs after a black woman, Rosa Parks, is imprisoned for refusing to pay a fine for sitting in a 'white' bus seat.

1962 The Commonwealth Electoral Act enables all Aboriginal Australians to vote.

1964 The Civil Rights Act (USA) prohibits discrimination of all kinds based on race, colour, religion, or national origin.

1965 The Commonwealth Racial Discrimination Act prohibits racial discrimination in the British Commonwealth.

1966 South Australia passes laws to end discrimination against Aboriginal people.

1968 Riots erupt around the USA at the assassination of black rights movement leader Martin Luther King.

1972 Dictator Idi Amin drives Asians out of Uganda. Many move to the UK, sparking racial tension.

1976 The Race Relations Act makes racial discrimination illegal in the UK.

1978 The US Supreme Court puts limits on affirmative action to prevent it damaging the rights of white people.

1993 Ethnic cleansing in Bosnia results in the enforced removal of around 1.5 million people for reasons of race or ethnic origin.

1994 Apartheid in South Africa ends with the election of Nelson Mandela as the first black president.

1994 Rwandan Hutu militia slaughter 800,000 Tutsi people.

1997 A ban on all affirmative action is passed in California, USA, making it illegal to discriminate against, or favour, anyone on the basis of race, sex, colour, ethnicity, or national origin.

2001 The World Conference against racism, racial discrimination, xenophobia and related intolerance is held in South Africa.

2005 The UK proposes laws allowing the deportation of foreigners thought to be promoting or glorifying terrorism or crime.

GLOSSARY

Aborigine A person descended from the original, black inhabitants of Australia.

affirmative action Giving special treatment to underprivileged groups to help them achieve equality.

apartheid The separation of black and white people in South Africa from 1948–1991.

asylum seeker A person who seeks to enter or stay in a different country because they claim they will be treated unfairly or harmed if they return to their own country.

Black Power movement A movement in the USA in the 1960s by black people rebelling against white oppression. Violent assaults occurred by both blacks and whites.

Caucasian Relating to white European heritage.

colonisation The process of taking over an area by settling there and exercising power over the inhabitants.

discrimination Treating people differently because of perceived difference, such as race.

ethnic cleansing The process of killing or removing all people of a particular national or racial group from an area.

genes The biological means by which inherited characteristics are passed on.

genocide The slaughter of an entire nationality or ethnic group.

ghetto An area of a city, often a slum, reserved for a particular group.

happy slapping Violence carried out while filming the attack with a camera phone.

Hasidic A branch of Judaism, begun in Eastern Europe in the eighteenth century, with a central belief that the realms of God and man are constantly in contact and interacting.

hierarchy A system with a graded order.

immigrant A person who has moved from one country to settle in another.

indigenous Originally inhabiting an area.

Ku Klux Klan A violent, anti-black, Christian organisation in the USA.

lynching Illegal killing, without trial, by suspending someone from a rope around the neck, often from a tree or lamp-post.

Nazi A member of the right-wing Nazi party in 1930s Germany.

neo-Nazi A member of an organisation that adopts Nazi ideas.

oppress To treat unfairly or cruelly.

racial quota A target set on the number of people from a race or ethnic group who will be recruited to a profession, job or college in the hope of redressing imbalance and giving people of different backgrounds a fair chance.

Roma Gypsies, originally from Slovakia or Romania.

segregation Division of people by colour, with people of different colours having to use different facilities.

supremacist A person who thinks that his or her group is best.

terrorism Illegal violence in pursuit of an aim, often political or religious.

RESOURCES

Books

Fiction

Skin Deep: A Collection of Stories About Racism
by Tony Bradman (editor) (Puffin Books, 2004)
Stories by established writers exploring the
roots of racism and racial conflict.

To Kill A Mocking Bird by Harper Lee (Harper
Collins, 2000. First published 1962)
The story of a young girl in the racist south of
the USA, confronting head-on the abuse of
black people.

Autobiography

Coming to England by Floella Benjamin
(Collins Educational, 2000)
The story of Floella Benjamin's move to
England from Trinidad.

Reference and non-fiction

Genocide by Sean Sheehan (Heinemann, 2005)
Presents the facts about genocide, for readers
aged 13+.

How do I Feel about Dealing with Racism?
by J Green (Franklin Watts, 2001)
Encourages readers to explore their own
feelings about race and racism; suitable for
younger readers.

Prejudice and Difference by Paul Wignall
(Heinemann Library, 2002)
Explores issues of prejudice that teenagers may
have, and offers ways of approaching them.

Racism **(21st century debates)** by Cathy
Senker (Raintree, 2003)
Combines a history of racism with accounts of
recent experiences.

Why Are People Racist? by Cathy Senker
(Hodder Wayland, 2002)
Explores the reasons for racism and what we
can do about it.

Websites

www.equalitytoday.org/
An online magazine dealing with racial issues
for young people.

www.zmag.org/racewatch/racewatch.cfm
A current affairs site focussing on race
problems, especially in the USA.

**http://web.channel4.com/learning/microsite
s/L/lifestuff/free_stuff.html**
Click on Try This://Citizenship to explore human
rights violations including racism in different
parts of the world.

**www.globalissues.org/HumanRights/
Racism.asp**
A comprehensive account of racism and related
issues all around the world.

INDEX